What Do Illustrators Do?

What Do Illustrators Do?

Written and Illustrated by

Eileen Christelow

INK

CLARION BOOKS/New York

Clarion Books
a Houghton Mifflin Company imprint
215 Park Avenue South, New York, NY 10003
Copyright © 1999 by Eileen Christelow
First Clarion paperback edition, 2007.

The illustrations for this book were executed in watercolor.
The text was set in 23/27-point Bembo.
www.clarionbooks.com
Printed in Malaysia

The Library of Congress has cataloged the hardcover edition as follows:
Christelow, Eileen.
What do illustrators do? / written and illustrated by Eileen Christelow.
p.   cm.
Summary: Shows two illustrators going through all the steps involved in creating new
picture books of "Jack and the Beanstalk," including layout, scale, and point-of-view.
ISBN: 0-395-90230-4
1. Illustration of books—Technique—Juvenile literature. 2. Jack and the beanstalk—
Illustrations—Juvenile literature. 3. Illustrated books, Children's—United States—
Juvenile literature. [1. Illustration of books. 2. Illustrators. 3. Book industries and
trade.] I. Title.   NC975.C46   1999   741.6´4—dc21   98-8297
CL ISBN–13: 978-0-395-90230-1   CL ISBN–10: 0-395-90230-4
PA ISBN–13: 978-0-618-87423-1   PA ISBN–10: 0-618-87423-2
TWP   15   14   13   12   11   10   9   8   7

4

What do illustrators do?
They tell stories with pictures.
 This picture shows where
two illustrators live and work.

Suppose those two illustrators each
decided to illustrate *Jack and the Beanstalk*.
Would they tell the story the same way?
Would they draw the same kind of pictures?

First, illustrators decide which scenes
in the story they want to illustrate . . .

A plan shows which pictures go on which pages.

After illustrators make a plan for their book, they need to make a **dummy**. (A dummy is a model of the book.) First they decide what shape and size the book will be.

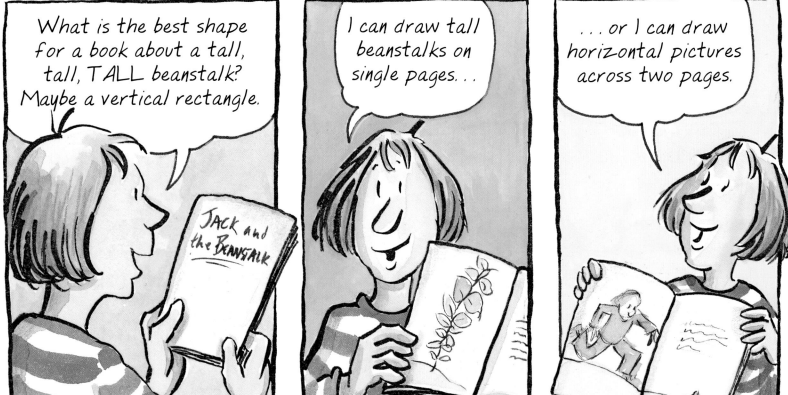

Then they make **sketches** of the pictures that will go on each page of the dummy.

The first sketches are often rough scribbles on tracing paper.

As they are sketching, illustrators need to decide how things will look: the characters, their clothes, the setting.

Illustrators can use their imaginations or they may have to do some research.

Some illustrators are also authors. They can change their story as they work on the sketches.

Each illustration has a different problem. For instance: From what **point of view** do you draw the magic bean being planted?

How do you draw a beanstalk
so it looks like it's growing?

There is usually more than one way to solve the same problem.

Here is another problem:
How do you make a beanstalk
look really TALL?

I could draw Jacqueline looking down the beanstalk...

...or looking up at it.

Things look so small when they are far away. Wait for me!

And things look bigger when they are close up.... That's called perspective.

Illustrators need to think about the design of each page.

Oops! If the giant doesn't look BIG enough or SCARY enough, the illustrator will draw that picture again.

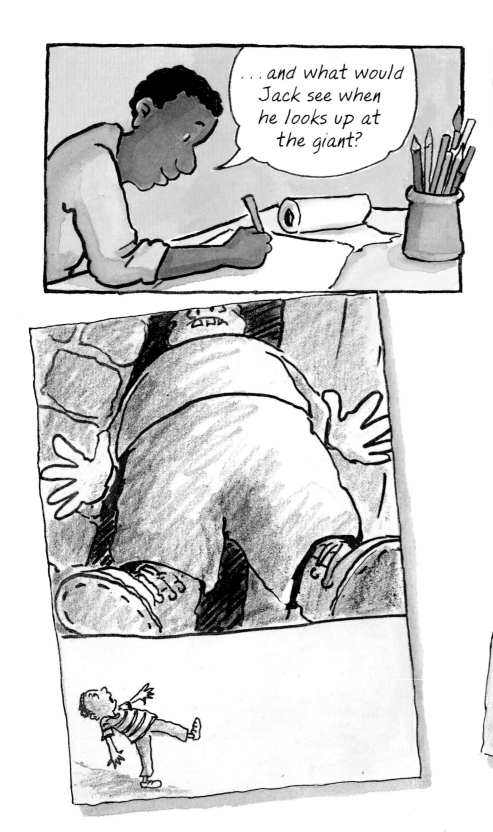

...and what would Jack see when he looks up at the giant?

These pictures are scarier! And we can only see part of the giant.

Which picture do you think he should use in the book?

How would it feel
to run across a table
right under the nose
of a sleeping GIANT?

Illustrators need to draw
how their characters feel.
(Sometimes they make
faces in a mirror to see how
an expression would look.)

Jacqueline tiptoed across the table. "Hurry up!" whispered the hen. "She never sleeps for long!"

Raised eyebrows?
Eyes wide open?
Mouth open?

Sometimes illustrators need someone else to model for them.

Each illustrator has a different **style** of drawing, just as every person has a different style of handwriting.

The giant . . . *Big Bob*

Jack . . . *Jack Trumper*

Jack's mom . . . *Ethel Trumper*

Jacqueline . . . *Jacqueline*

Different styles for drawing Jack and Jacqueline

We're trying a new style.

When illustrators have finished
their dummies, they show them
to the editor and the designer at the
publishing company.

The editor decides whether the
pictures tell the story.

The designer makes suggestions about the design of the book.

She chooses the typeface for the words and the cover.

I think the book could be a little bigger.

I'd love that!

I'm sending you the type. I hope you like it.

Sample typefaces for title:

Jack and the Beanstalk

Jack and the Beanstalk

Jack and the Beanstalk

Sample typefaces for text:

(easy to read)

While Jacqueline slept in her bedroom below, the magic bean grew . . . and grew . . .

(not so easy to read)

While Jacqueline slept in her bedroom below, the magic bean grew . . . and grew . . .

What do you think of this typeface?

I can't read a thing you are saying.

Illustrators need to decide how they want to do the finished illustrations. They can draw different kinds of lines and textures with different kinds of tools.

pencil

pen with flexible point

brush

felt tip pen

They can color their illustrations with paint, pastels, pencils, or crayons. . .

watercolors

watercolor crayons

colored pencils

They can do an illustration without any black line at all!

Illustrators need to choose the paper they want to use for their finished illustrations.

Some papers are good for watercolor, others for pastel, others for pencil... Some are smooth. Some are textured.

Illustrators go to art stores to buy their supplies.

Illustrators often use a lightbox to trace their drawings onto their new paper.

33

Sometimes illustrators
throw away their pictures
and start again.

Sometimes they change the colors.

Too many cool colors! Blue flowers, blue shoes, green leaves.

I need to add some warm colors - reds, oranges, yellows.

Well, maybe not that many!

Cool colors make you feel cool, calm, relaxed or sometimes sad.

Warm colors make you feel bright, wild, loud, red hot!

Or they may change the composition.

It can take months to finish all the illustrations for a picture book.

Before they are sent to the publisher, they need to be checked to make sure nothing is left out.

Illustrators often do the cover of the book last. The cover tells a lot about a story: What is it about? Does it look interesting?

The cover is a clue to how the illustrator will tell the story. Would these covers make you want to read the books?

This illustration tells how the two illustrators
celebrated when they finally finished all that work!